# Love's

## A N S W E R

Winner of the Iowa Poetry Prize

# Love's

## A N S W E R

Poems by **MICHAEL HEFFERNAN**

University of Iowa Press ᴪ Iowa City

University of Iowa Press, Iowa City 52242

Printed in the United States of America

Design by Richard Hendel

Printed on acid-free paper

Library of Congress Cataloging-in-Publication Data

Heffernan, Michael, 1942–

    Love's answer: poems / by Michael Heffernan.

      p.   cm.—(The Iowa Poetry Prize)

    ISBN 0-87745-451-5 (pbk.)

    I. Title.  II. Series.

    PS3558.E413L68   1994

    811'.54 —dc20                93-38321

                                    CIP

98  97  96  95  94  P  5  4  3  2  1

*For Mick, Jim, Joe, and Kathy*

*and in memory of my father and mother,*

*Joseph and Susan Heffernan*

Deliver my soul from the sword;

my darling from the power of the dog.

Psalm 22:20

# CONTENTS

## ACKNOWLEDGMENTS

The author thanks the editors of the following journals where these poems first appeared, sometimes in earlier versions:

*Chariton Review*: "The Monks at Large," "A Passerby and His Companions Visit the Widow after the Mad Avenger's Dreadful Accident," and "Remembering Skye"

*Crazyhorse*: "On the Beach at Saugatuck"

*Cyphers* (Ireland): "The Abyss" and "The Atonement"

*Gettysburg Review*: "The Atonement," "Badia Fiesolana," "The Blessings of Liberty," "The Light of the Living," "Truth," and "Watering Impatiens"

*Iowa Review*: "Angelology," "Lawn Mower," "A Light in the House," and "A Phantom of Delight"

*Kentucky Poetry Review*: "Merciless Beauty"

*New Criterion*: "Magpies" and "The World of Light"

*North American Review*: "The Facts on the Ground"

*Plains Poetry Journal*: "The Council"

*Poetry Northwest*: "The Last Man," "This Life," and "Why We Forget the Things We Thought We Wouldn't"

*The Quarterly*: "The Ape of Emain Macha," "The Banquet," "B-Minor Mass," "The Consolation," "Dream Vacation," "The Flesh," "A Highway Brook in Dingle," "The Island," "The Land of Heart's Desire," "Lost Boy," "The Magnum Opus," "The Nightgown," "The Peasants' Rising," "The Queen of Heaven," "Rendering Aquinas," "A Rhetoric upon the Window," "The Rooming House," "Souls in Purgatory," "A State of Grace," and "Summer in Umbria"

*Shenandoah*: "A Catch in the Breath," "A Girl Sings to Moravia at the World's End," and "The Moving Statue at Melleray"
*Sycamore Review*: "A Sign from Heaven"
*Tar River Poetry*: "The Boulevardier" and "Lake Isle"
*Willow Springs*: "Café Paradiso," "The Music of Forgiveness," "Requiem," and "A Temptation in the Wilderness"

This book's completion was assisted by fellowship grants from the National Endowment for the Arts, the Arkansas Arts Council, and An Chomhairle Ealaíon/The Arts Council, Ireland.

1

A monk rowed out to sea in a boat no bigger
than the pallet he left behind in his tiny cell.
Light as a wafer it wobbled over the waves.
The box with his belongings had lost its lid
and left his wake awash with loveletters.
Just beyond sight of land he raised the oars
and crossed them at his feet and said his prayers.
The One Who Is More Than Being filled his soul
with nothingness no intellect could perceive
except the one that formed it in the first place.
He spilled his mind into the mind of God.
Visions of women in nothing more than towels
bent to anoint him. Grabbing at the oars,
he pulled the sea back over what he had prayed.

## THE FACTS ON THE GROUND

Neither an object of terror nor wonder,
though very beautiful as any vision
out of the old Arcadian delusion,
the half-moon suddenly stood from a pillar

of fiery light arising in the water,
and it was this spectacle that I dwelt on
hard as I might for a good long time, and then
turned back within, where things kept their own order

all to themselves, so different from the moon,
but scarcely like us either, though they partook
of us, yet every one belonging to none

and sundry, in their peculiar bailiwick,
where trouble of every kind went up and down,
no matter what light brightened or what man spoke.

## A TEMPTATION IN THE WILDERNESS

Whatever Bernard of Clairvaux thought he saw
in his valley of clear light as the beechwood caught
the sun's declension leaving a bowl of fire
with every trunk a candle offering prayer

so that, while night came on, a scent of smoke would rise
as of wicks pinched out and a waxen stench to the nose—
it wasn't for him to know whether this was God's
own chosen home for the soul astray in the body,

nor could he make out much of what this was,
except to invoke that voluptuous metaphor
from the Song of Songs: the Bridegroom and the Bride

preparing their mouths for kisses on the way to bed,
which is the sun's face languidly leaning westward,
and a shiver of limbs, and torrents of golden hair.

On into spring, around St. Anselm's day,
I take another look at the Redemption,
and first I ask, What is there to redeem?

What have I done but fall into this flesh
which is the way it is because it is
and not because of something someone did

to That-Than-Which-None-Greater-Can-Be-Conceived—
which is a phraseology I admired,
and admired Professor Quinn for saying it

the spring of '62 in that lecture hall
with casement windows hung on the musky breeze
bloody and bosomy and rank with love

and not God's love but Beverly Doherty's,
who drove men mad on her front porch in the lamplight
to be at one with parts of her she kept

untouchable behind her father's door,
shutting out all but the last smell of her
under the nostril in the sweet night air.

The woman in beige slacks walking her dog
has certainly walked around the block more than once
since I first saw her fifteen minutes ago

up the sidewalk in the next street over
from where she lives. Her dog is off-white,
almost a kind of beige. The same cloudcover covers them

that covers me. I am a ten-minute walk away.
I have no dog to walk, only a cat to watch,
who sits with his tail tucked under

and his free throat fearlessly poised upon the air.
He too is mostly beige. He watches the gossamer
filaments laden with pods that cling to the breeze

and waits for the pageantry of his life to begin.
I wish I could say, with only a soupçon
of sprezzatura, that I knew full well that she

who was walking her dog could never think about me
or about whether the beige radiance over our bed
would glimmer a little like gold before we slept.

## THE LIGHT OF THE LIVING

Trying to see the work of the eye
in what the eye was trying to see,

I went to where my eyes were,
where the inmost eye in the middle of me

looked out and found the sun on fire.
Birds fell from the sky like freezing rain.

Though it was summer, deep summer, deep
indolent summer, ice fell off treelimbs,

breaking into pieces in thunder; then,
sooner than I expected, spring came—

intimate, comely, viridescent spring;
and so I strayed off into the air.

Two blind black angels hungry for home
climbed from the corners of my eyes.

## ANOTHER PART OF THE FOREST

The mirror's image of the window
with its sprucetips in cerulean

puts pieces of that world beside
this piece of me. The mind within

the face the mirror faces says
There is a tall green shape against

the primal blue aglimmer with itself
abounding in the roots of silence.

Treetops keep quiet counsel.
I bring my face under the pane

and look. By God it's bright there
in the neighborhood of fellow men

gathering twigs from the wilderness
on the darksides of spruces.

There was a life outside of this one, which
the Old Ones told us was the one that was.
Guidance came freely but was often wrong.
Then mischievous Brother Malachy observed
that the greatest obstacle to godliness
worth breeching was the buckle at the waist
of a girl like Nora Doyle in Cornavogue.
Sniggering at that against our better judgment,
we nonetheless felt sure the man was right.
Where did it say there wasn't someplace else
for men to meet the truth that made them free?
If lives like ours were even feasible
to start with—if the keepers of the Faith
would keep it, were there any faith to keep—
we could have had good reason to take up
this type of work, if work was what this was.
Meantime, outside the wall, a pair of magpies
tumbled above the ditch along the road.
We stood to watch them. Father Bernard begged
the Mother of Christ to shut her face from us,
as we stepped out down a path of mottled shade
into a field of girlish marigolds.

His craving for the flesh of Mary Quinlan
had faded softly into dumb disuse.
Now and again he walked down the boreen
beside her cottage in the aspen copse,
and he could draw up from his soul the dream
of moss as bright as ginger among her thighs
where he could leap like a great frog after a rain.
The way in was a low path under branches,
and there were nettles in the ditch beside,
but Mary Quinlan sang to the sweet winds
that nudged the curtains at the kitchen window
where he might see her shadow in the lace
or take her song and carry it on his way
up to the bridge to croon it to the river.
A gang of blackbirds bickered from the poplars.
One Friesian uttered forth a burst of spray,
blessing the buttercups. He kept on singing.
The sound rose like a noise among the nations,
a lovecry from the heart's embitterment,
the loin's remorse for sweetness kept away,
where gray walls showed the Virgin and her child
a blue fly on the lampshade by the bed.

## THIS LIFE

I get in the car. This is that moment when
the moment later on when I will turn
into the driveway flashes into mind
and I know for certain I will live at least that long.
I drive down Dickson Street thinking about this,
until I am distracted by the girl in the white sweater
on the corner near the Boardwalk Café:
I realize again, as I do every day,
what truly matters in this life, what is apart
from time and its monstrosity. She gets in the car.
We are driving down the coast road south of Genoa,
heading for Leghorn. She has just stopped laughing
at one of my remarks about her legs
and my horns and is staring at the sea.

I hadn't quite realized I had died
before the man in the plaid pants came in
to ask the way to the bathroom and we went
together down an alley in the old neighborhood

where little Mrs. Ferris was holding up
her lost cat's collar and she said You sons
of bitches put this pussy in the sky
I know you did, and I said this was true

while Al over here was numb with glee to think
it could have meant that much at all
to two such desperadoes as the likes of us
if they had Pussy in Paradise.

After our luncheon of yak-brain potpie,
I turned to Tonya, who had nothing on
but a pewter crucifix between her breasts,
a thumb's breadth from the plump rim of her navel.
A dying Jesus in a place like that
adduced the natural proximity
of bodily and godly sacrament.
I was a warrior-king in yak-skin breeches,
kneeling before her. She lifted the cross of Christ
over her shoulders and flung it onto the bed.
Then she grabbed both her hands behind my ears
and led my face into a hinterland
where briny winds blew over me till I heard
voices from kingdoms no man could leave alive.

What Richard Nixon said at the Great Wall
bears paraphrasing here: It's a great lake.
I must have died and gone to Saugatuck.
The children dig for China. Several
of the more radiantly animal
natures recumbent everywhere I look
have given up the ghost or taken back
bodies more ancient than the wakened soul.
Instead of China, what the children find
are graves to bury one another in.
They look like ashen warriors when they rise.
I'd like to take them with me by the hand
to rinse them in these waters so they shine,
plainly proclaiming how great the light is.

The door was shut. I opened and came in.
Two windows to one side were likewise shut.
I stood beside the bare wall opposite.

With any luck at all, I might have stayed
beside that wall all day, but then the door
swung on its hinges like a broken arm.

Something was happening that I did not like.
I can remember bringing the door to
and turning with a question in my mind

about the Whole Shebang and what's behind it
and whether this was the Lord that had come in
to keep me company in my wonderment

or judge me with the living and the dead,
but then the wall broke open and the floor
fell out from under. I was standing barefoot

wearing a pair of avocado knickers,
fuchsia suspenders and a blue paisley shirt,
blossoming in the middle of thin air.

Regarding what has already been said
about the pathetic way most people are
in this place, it's hard not to take into account
the strong point made about the presence of dogs
in nearly everyone's backyard, and also
the interesting conclusions someone drew,
I believe it was the gentleman in the bolo tie,
about the preference for beige automobiles
and painted pale blue face-brick on the houses,
all of which points to spiritual disquiet
manifesting itself in measures of abeyance
taken to ease the sense of life on the edge,
or under siege from forces meant to kill.
I'd recommend we get this on the agenda
for next month's meeting. Meanwhile we should try
and think about what the rest of us might suggest
to correct the problem. Before we adjourn,
let's thank Arlene for the hard work she did
putting the program together, and especially
for the lovely table favors, which she made herself.

## A PASSERBY AND HIS COMPANIONS VISIT THE WIDOW AFTER THE MAD AVENGER'S DREADFUL ACCIDENT

We thought it was safe enough to come in here.
At least they did. I didn't, but that's me.
I am the one that wants it in the papers,
if not the encyclopedia, but at least
in writing, that the mayhem is history
and the coast is clear. I came along regardless
to look in with them and to answer questions.
These people go by feeling, not by sight.
They asked me would I like to bring them over.
I wasn't occupied, so I said I would.
Amid the big din and the heat and havoc,
I watched your man flung up above the roof,
then back down like the proverbial rag doll.
I'm glad he wasn't anyone I knew.
I guess the part that burned can be repaired.
They say they'd like to help you clean this up.
They work well for blind people. Give them brooms,
show them the way to the trashcans in the alley,
they'll go to work and clean this mess right up,
including your man in the yard, although the birds
apparently made off with most of him,
the way it looks from here. I'm glad they came
to get me, really. It is times like these
only your neighbors know what's necessary.

Night after night I dreamed about hotels,
mostly the same one, with a thousand rooms,
in one of which I left all of my clothes
and in another someone that I loved,
while in a third my own distracted self,
whose odd persona I had never met,
was looking for a way to take a shower,
facing a rack of suits in an old armoire
that I imagined was a shower stall,
with a woman entering from the fire escape
to find her husband underneath the bed
while this demented man who stared at her
from behind the shivering door of an old armoire
was only looking for a decent room
somewhere around this dull arrondissement
at one of any number of plain hotels
that cater to backpackers or wayward priests
on holiday with young girls from the parish
or men like him in search of who knows what
that leads them into streets with gray façades
and double doors revealing passageways
emptying into courtyards where cupids leap
on one foot over bursts of pearly spray
besprinkling the sun's imperial countenance.

Invite them in to where they take you over,
any of them who happen to have seen
the way you looked askance at them, enough
to mind it. They were only too well aware
of dissolute black corners in the cellars
of your gelatinous depravity, complete
with cobwebs and milky drool. Custom holds,
in these parts anyhow, that who one knows
means everything, but only if
the priests determine that a holy wind
fondled the top fronds of the bristlepalms
at the exact moment of that person's birth
you sought the aid of, under flights of swans.
You gave me words I would have loved to have
for my support group, or the ladies in
the Lyric Relief Guild, home truths more poignant
and more rife with wild complaint
than the usual mindfuck. A tropical brightness
sweltered and grew thin. Trouble that fell
on everyone was all one kind of trouble.
At least we knew we were supposed to know that
and to try to do something to take care of it,
even on such an abject afternoon
in the middle of any number of broken lives
mended by all the good word we could get
to filter through to us over assumed names.

# THE BANQUET

A hallway bigger than most people's houses
awaited me in the next to last episode.
At the end of it a massive double door
opened on the Duke of Tuscany at table
attended by naked dwarves. I stayed outside
to watch the evening play through the draperies
at the farther end of the hall where I came from,
with its enormous doorways quiet as caverns.
I knew there were councillors in the anteroom
full of news even I could deliver with aplomb,
but the lord was at table in the midst of his joy,
made much of, whispered to, kept in regard
by persons whose bodies fed from his own.
Behind me other doors were wobbling shut.
I knew if I walked in to where the great man was,
my soul no longer would be mine to save.
Glory and madness dwelt in the one room.
The way my shoulders turned when I looked back
was like a wall that stood behind my eyes
and echoed with the good loud noise I made.

I can't believe I am telling this again.
When he came back that night, he had a load
of answers, as he put it, and he knew
why I was angry with him that whole time.
He walked in with a wild look in his eye,
wilder than any I had ever seen,
on him or anybody, drunk or sober,
and he was mainly sober, though with a look
and with a way of lunging through the door
as if he had been pushed in by some thing
that stood behind him in the dark outside.
He said he got here in one piece, the way
I told him he would have to if he came home;
and he had not been drunk, more than halfway,
before I found him as I found him then,
trembling and weeping, rubbing at his face
with both his wrists, both of them slick with tears
and shoved out from the sleeves of his good coat
so his elbows almost popped through at the cuffs;
and in the midst of this he was telling me
he hadn't any right to anyone's
forgiveness, and the things he spent his life
doing to me were unforgivable.
I wished I knew what he was getting at
or what he'd done to me that was that bad.
Later that week I saw the last of him.
We sat at the far end of the Fifth Floor

away from all the others, for his sake:
he said he was embarrassed, still, to be there.
Everything had at last come clear to him:
he had written down the answers he came home with
in a book about my anger—how my anger
was the power that drove the planets around the sun,
and he had come to be in tune with it,
he said, which was the reason why he hummed
so much, and bothered people with his humming—
he understood that now, but couldn't stop,
and so the last thing that I heard him do
was hum whatever melody that was—
if it was even music—that he hummed
and kept on humming. I can hear him now,
the way I always hear him when I tell you this.

Early in the winter of the year 1312, the monks of the Cistercian abbey of Fossanuova took the body of Thomas Aquinas, who had died there in March of 1274, and boiled the flesh from the bones, in order to place them in a small casket that could be moved from hiding place to hiding place, so great was their fear of the Dominicans of Toulouse, the brethren of Thomas Aquinas, and so deep was their love for the Angelic Doctor, who had chosen this monastery as the place to die, giving them the right, so they thought, to keep his bones forever in their care. A quantity of flesh remained, after all those years, since Thomas Aquinas had been a corpulent man, who had died in the odor of sanctity. A first unearthing of the corpse, by these same jealous Cistercians, for the purpose of moving it to a place of greater seclusion, revealed the corpse to be still incorrupt. When they took the remains up out of the chapel floor, a sweet air spilled forth from under the coffin lid. On that occasion, the abbot James of Ferentino appointed three monks to exhume the body and decapitate it. The head was placed in a metal box and immured in a corner of the chapel. A time afterward, in the early winter of the year 1312, both head and trunk were boiled. The monks prepared two cauldrons for the purpose, one for the severed arms and legs of Thomas Aquinas, along with the head from its metal box in the chapel, and the other for the great mass of gut and heart. The left hand had already been removed, in 1288, by Aquinas' sister, the Countess Theodora of Sanseverino, whereas the right thumb had been taken, shortly after death, by Aquinas' secretary and companion, Reginald of

Piperno. The boiling took place behind the chapel, in the monastery courtyard, in the open air, a few paces in the direction of the pigsty. The steam that lifted in billows to the ashen sky carried in it an aroma like that of seasoned venison. One of the attending monks later claimed that he had indeed placed two large sprigs of finochio in the bubbling cauldrons. An oily vapor breathed lightly over the cheeks of the monks around the cauldrons as they rubbed their elbows against the early winter chill. An old monk marching briskly through the courtyard on his way to Vespers took a deep breath and muttered something about the lavishness of the fare being prepared for the abbot's table. Monks wearing sturdy leather gloves pushed staves against the cauldrons and upended their contents onto the ground. The bones were allowed to cool and were then gathered into a crate and carried into the rear of the sacristy. What was left of the flesh was buried at the site where the cauldrons had stood. A cat came stepping out from the monastery's grain bin to poke her nose where the juice of Aquinas lay soaking in the earth among cinders and clods of clay. From his place near the pigsty, Brother Bonifacio watched as the cat's tongue lapped at an islet of fatty film on one of several puddles. Brother Bonifacio lifted a pitchfork from its peg. He took the pitchfork in both hands. He crept up carefully behind the cat. Just as she raised her head to lick the smudge from the hairs of her upper lip, the monk pushed the pitchfork between her shoulders.

Since it is open and the world is blue,
I want to know why God's face can't be there,
watching me from the yard beyond the window.
Brothers and sisters, I have been trying hard
to find him, and I know you say you know
precisely where it happens we should look,
which isn't anywhere near my backyard.
I can't help asking why he can't be there,
unless he is and I'm not seeing him
for something in my eye that's in the way
or something in my brain that makes him fade
as soon as what I see goes through the nerve
and comes out on the other end a blur,
a scrambled message that the brain can't keep
because of what I put there in the way.
The mind goes blind as surely as the eye—
but what if suddenly I am proven wrong
and there he is, an enormous hummingbird,
gathering the air around him as he raises
his winged face and everything else with him,
taking me through the window into light
as quickly as he came, and there I am,
rapt in the radiance with nothing left
but blue as blue as all there is of blue—
what if that happened and this poem came true?—
with the blank space or the stillness afterward
like daylight emptied of the one hummingbird.

2

I used to sit down drunk on my front porch
to watch the afternoon and the mulberry

mingle together with timbrels and dances
to the windchime's ruthless tinkle, as if the sun

could leap and kick his heels around that tree
in her small gown of green, beside the shadow

because it was not the light I wanted there,
but other light that stood among cypresses

beyond a garden with figtrees and cicadas
jangling above the voices of young girls

who stopped to take their shoes off by the gate
so they could dance home barefoot from there on.

Shouldering my knapsack over the Forth Bridge,
I shoved a thumb into the wind and gullcry.
An early lorryman carried me to Perth
through fields of barley dappled with cloudy light.

From the edge of Perth I rode with Jimmy Thompson,
who said he was driving to the Isle of Skye.
"I'm on my way to Inverness," I told him.
"It's a bleak road to Inverness that way,
with hardly any traffic past Kingussie,
so you may want to forgo Inverness," he said.

Kingussie was a few huts in a valley.
Dark ribbons of peat-smoke were all that moved
in that place, so I stayed in Jimmy's car
for the wild journey through the Highlands to the Isles.

All I remember of the Isle of Skye
are long white roads among the Cuillin Hills,
an old man speaking Erse beside a gate,
Sam Johnson's portrait at Dunvegan Castle,
and a rank fire in Kyleakin at the pub
where I watched the signboard shaking in the rain.

# THE APE OF EMAIN MACHA

The king at Emain Macha had an ape
which someone brought to him from Africa.
This was a Barbary ape, whose skull was found
when the great mound was opened, along with brooches,
trumpets, other bones of pigs and cattle—
nothing unusual, except for the ape's skull,
and a man's skull, also, severed down the middle.

I lay on top of that great dome over Ulster,
and watched two blackbirds drifting near the sun.
They made a pair of rings one on the other.
I heard the roar of the king's boy-warriors
striving with Cuchulain on the Armagh road.
The king's ape leaped and screamed with terrible joy
to see the blood of children spilt for fun.

Traveling the coast road from Ventry to Slea Head,
    we came to a place where the blacktop
stops by a brook rushing down from the mountain
    over stones replacing the highway,
providing us both miracle and hazard,
    with a thought for the County Council
and how they could countenance such a marvel—

as well as a thought for the cliff's edge just there
    to one side of us, frighteningly
hidden by the roadside wall and swollen turf.
    We scarcely thanked God for good weather.
Mist would at least obscure the terrible plunge.
    We had no choice but to go on through.
Halfway over, we stopped and opened the doors

to pick up glistening stones for souvenirs.
    The water rattling from above us
purled and winked and murmured underneath. Below,
    the ocean spoke in tones oceans use.
Old gods might be staring from behind the light
    at this intersection of known worlds,
while the human roadway rose to carry us.

The Virgin stood alone in her shady niche
and would not move, although the light would move
among the rusty beeches, offering to splash
her whiteness with blots of starker white. Above,
the sun looked very lively, but the lady
kept herself quiet, with her palms together,
a ring of stars over her brow, her body
muted under the gown she wore, or rather
that someone formed her in. A loud man prayed
ahead of seven others at their prayers,
all of them groaning in the greenlit glade
about their sins and keeping away from fires,
but Mary made no motion. Water spilled
from a pipe into a pool that was black and cold.

## POULNABRONE DOLMEN

They buried the old king under this capstone
after they carved his brain out with a shell
and broiled the rest of him, wrapping his bones
in elkskin, once the god devoured his soul
and the priests had eaten his brain uncooked,
passing the bits among them on a stick.
The burial was covered under a mound of earth
which gradually disappeared, leaving these stones
with absolutely no sign of a man at all.
When I drove down here once, around midsummer,
I found a great rock bird about to fly,
until I noticed fistfuls of recent rain
all over the capstone, while the one wren
that had come to drink took off into the country.

## LAKE ISLE

There was in the likelihood of being taken
by purple shadows over the still water
and the curlew's cry across it from the island
with its ivied remnant of a tower wall
subsiding near a few ministerial elms
a risk I knew I faced all on my own
under a sky releasing whiffs of breeze
that cooled my brow and loosed the thought of home
like a waftage of lavender from dresser drawers
opened by fingers I had dreamed of kissing
the morning there were voices in the hedge
and a pathway wandering into the garden's heart
the cry of whose one bird would make a shadow
that fled like a wintry call over black water.

Once I had found my way out of Dublin
one grimy Friday afternoon at rush hour,
I came to Kilkenny with its steamy fields
and Tipperary under a choking haze,
having passed by the Rock of Dunamase
just off the main road I was driving on,
where I might rest my back against a stone
and dream about the wood-owl's darkening call
across the valley from the aspen grove.
A wave of blackbirds rose up to a wire
and settled in a row. I came to Cashel,
giving the Rock of Cashel half a look,
then drove to Cahir to the Cahir House Hotel
and took a room on the top floor well above
the rattle and roar of lorries in the square,
along with the noise of the band in the ballroom
which the desk clerk told me would play that night,
and probably loudly, to a late hour.
I said I wouldn't mind it, being tired,
intending to get to bed more or less directly,
which I did not do. Instead, I walked around,
and stopped to watch a heron in the Suir
beside the Castle, stepping carefully
among the stones, oblivious of me
or even of the traffic on the bridge,
till I succumbed to hunger like the bird's
and bought myself a bag of fish-and-chips

to dine on while I walked around the square.
I threw the paper bag in a trashcan
and walked up to the menubox by the door
of the Galtee Inn, to see how much the nightlife
could cost a man in Cahir. I went inside.
The barmaid was a girl I thought I knew
eleven years ago, and there she was,
lifting glasses by the rim three at a time
over the same bar she played under as a child,
ducking among the lunch-crowd on their stools.
One of the forms of grace we learn about
involves the avoidance of nostalgia
and other mysticalities men are given to,
making them stop and stand and rub their arms
with a lost look as if the feast were done
and the last guest were rising to go home.
If anyone was watching, it might have seemed
that that was what I did for a small time,
standing to one side, till it came to me
that no one in the room, including her,
would care that someone all but lost in joy
had walked in out of the evening to stand there
among townspeople other than his own,
taking a weekend's ease. As I walked out,
though there was light enough to see her by,
the heron had found a new place in the river.

Moravia appeared on Inishmore
one sunlit evening with his entourage—
two women and a glib photographer.
It was an odd place for Moravia.
The girls at Bridget Hernon's came to the gate,
as I walked up from the sunset at Bungowla,
to tell me Alberto Moravia had arrived
and he was in the parlor beside the fire
being sung to by a village girl in Irish,
with his silver-handled cane beside his knee,
under Oscar Wilde's grandfather's portrait
with the same chin and forehead as Oscar Wilde's,
as Bridget Hernon pointed out to us
while stirring coals and setting some turf in
for what appeared to be a bad turn in the weather
according to the forecast on the TV,
as well as a lost chance for Moravia
to see Dún Aengus, which the photographer
had no idea was only a short walk away,
a few fields up the hill behind the house,
though altogether beyond Moravia's
bad legs and ventricles. The girl's keening song
rose sharply on the warm air of the room.
After the silence came when she was done,
we all said "Brava" but Moravia,
who tapped the silver handle of his cane,
shaped to resemble a waterbird of some kind

with a long beak like a gull's or a cormorant's
and a half-smile like the one Moravia gave
instead of "Brava" for the girl's heartbreaking song,
the gist of which she tried to explain to us,
and the photographer, who had good English,
passed this along to Moravia, who nodded
and blinked his eyes under his great eyebrows
but said precisely nothing in reply.
The girl began to sing another song,
that came from a joke the kelpers used to tell
in the eighteenth century. She didn't know
the point of it herself, but she liked to sing it
because it had a lovely leaping tune,
and when she finished it, we all said "Brava,"
while Moravia wrapped his hand around the beak
of the silver gull or cormorant and moved his cane
in what seemed another gesture of approval,
except this time he pulled himself to his feet,
bent in a kind of wavering bow to us,
nodded his head to the girl, and left the room.
One of the women turned to me and said,
"Alberto is very tired." Bridget came back
to pick up the tea-things and to make it known
that the purple sunset meant fair weather tomorrow,
despite the television's foul prediction.
I said I hoped Signor Moravia
at least could see Dún Aengus from a distance,

if not go up to it. I knew a boreen
off the main road south of Corrúch near Oatquarter
that led along the north side of the ridge
until Dún Aengus came into plain view,
but the boreen was rocky, and besides
I liked the way it seemed to belong to me
the afternoon I'd found it and gone down
to where Dún Aengus suddenly was there,
looking about to slide into the sea,
across the valley among choughs and bees.
The Italians all were on their way to bed.
They had brought Moravia to the world's end
but could not carry him to the edge of it
to lean above the wailing kittiwakes
for one last look at the long drop out of here,
or to tighten his hold around a waterbird
that would lead him back to listen beside the fire.

# MAGPIES

My friend has come home from a week in Lourdes
between treatments at the Cork Cancer Hospital.
She says it's wonderful what they're doing now
to keep us all alive. But something always
is out for us, don't you think? she wonders,
waiting to get us, I mean, don't you think?
Sadness surprises me as I watch her hands
lifting her thought in the air and letting it go
like a magpie leaping a ditch into a meadow.
Through the window behind her, a quick light shines
among elderberry bushes with their lacy disks
turned to the wolfpack sky above the vale.
Pastoral, she says, this place is a pastoral place,
the way we used to imagine the afterlife.
But there is no afterlife, she tells me then.
Even in Ireland, we have doubts about all that.
We live here now; and afterwards, most likely,
the magpies come to leap over the ditches.

Eriugena caught the sound of God
coming to him one night from a lost moon
that hid itself behind a drumlin wood
not long before the sun came back again.
This was the music light makes over Ireland,
as jackdaws toss themselves like chips of slate
over gray lake water under a smear of sky,
their cursive wingbeats writing nothing down.
Maybe he thought this was the song God made
the night the moon came out for the first time
to put light in the place of that much sky
that otherwise was dark without the moon.
All this is set forth in a book he wrote
in the ninth century for the king of France,
who never understood a thing he meant,
but sat and drank and watched the moon go down
just before cockcrow, a long way from Ireland.

Whatever else we did or could have done,
or tried to think of when the time had come,
would always bring us to this place of stone,
cold and forgetfulness. There was the same
pain in our hearts as we would often have,
enough to mourn by, and in mourning thus,
we surely came to know the end of love,
its purpose and its only terminus.
And so we all were as we were before,
wanting to make of it what we could bear,
but realizing even so the lies
we liked to hear, about the galaxies,
and how the dead would send back light from them
more like a song than any requiem.

*for Martha*

## THE MAGNUM OPUS

The king had inquired
about the progress
of the Magnum Opus.

I sent back word
of my investigation
into the variance of hue

between the color
on the upper side
and the color
on the underside

of a mulberry leaf
teetering
in the least
of evening breezes.

At a table by the window I laid a spoon
beside a cup and found myself in a café
where the napkin under the spoon read Vichy-État
and a woman on the street was about to ask me
"Cherchez-vous l'amour?" to which I would reply
that I had left the one love of my life
by herself at the hotel, though here she was
offering me everything she thought I wanted
in Paris in the blue air of a dream
of woven brick streets dappled by leaf shadow
as girls walked arm in arm by the shop windows.

We stood there on that bridge above the river
halfway across it from the Quai d'Orléans
one morning in September, having come
just then from the Gare de l'Est where the train had left us
looking like Rumanian émigrés—
at least I felt like one, in my filthy coat
I slept in for four days. I wish I remembered
what she was wearing, what she said to me,
what I said back to her, what we thought went wrong,
but none of this comes clear after all these years,
and besides I am positive it does not matter.
There is an exactitude that shapes our ends
however much we labor to displace them.
The thing that brings this lump into the gullet
every time I try to bring it back
the way it was that morning by the Seine
is something I forget the way it was
the way it is when it comes back to me
odd moments by myself around the house
or going along about my daily life
when suddenly I could be breaking into song
and it would be that song I sang alone
waiting for the Métro at the Place des Vosges,
which was the song that came to me long after that
this morning at the post office, where a woman
walking toward me in the same blue coat she wore,
bent over the railing by the Quai d'Orléans,
could whisper to me something unforgettable.

## DREAM VACATION

We leave the children at their uncle's place,
live for two weeks on the train from London
to Istanbul and back, by way of Paris,
Munich, Vienna, Budapest, and Athens,
including a sea voyage down to Crete
to sit on Minos' alabaster throne,
the locusts roaring in a door of light,
the dusty bus back to Iráklion,
an empty wine bottle thrown in the ship's wake,
Piraeus by dawn, the second-class coach at noon.

The children, at the uncle's pleasure palace,
learn to play blackjack with his lady friend.
She's glad to be with someone else's kids.
The days flow by around the swimming pool.
He brings home pizza, videos, diet Coke.
The privacy fence keeps water like a jewel
and leaping bodies, while the sky above
is the same sky that covers the Aegean
in the other life all of us go on living,
by pools of light, in bodies lit with love.

What could we want from Johann Sebastian
but to slow down for the Crucifixion,
then raise the roof with Jesus Risen?
That melodrama was a way of telling
what music would have us take from mystery
before we came to find out otherwise—
stopping where faith begins, bringing the truth
down from among those rafters rent with song.
I keep on hearing something else again,
the Crucifixion's joy, the Rising's terror,
Nature's relentless will to do us harm,
then leave us humming snatches of a tune
we lost the words for, while the morning light
sang from above to taunt us as we mourned.

Look to the blue above the neighborhood,
and nothing there gives any help at all.
We have seen the fuchsia, and it doesn't work.
Time flows away. The mystery it fills
with our undoing moves aside awhile
and brings a new reality into play,
apparently—and here is the main idea:
the wind of time appears to blow through here,
the periwinkle and the mayapple
trembling in wind that is of their own kind,
a gorgeous color of a clarity
that fills our eyes with brightness to see through,
for all the good it does us, and to tell
the morning glory from the glory of God.

Wat Tyler killed King Richard's tax collector
with a roofer's hammer. The man tried to prove
Wat's daughter old enough to pay the tax.
The girl sat shucking peas beside the fire.
The tax collector dragged her by the elbows
and tore her clothes off. "Woman flesh I call this,"
he roared. Wat Tyler's hammer went to work.
From collarbone to forehead Wat was a fire.
The girl's pale skin dripped brains and bits of skull.
A growling rabble gathered at the window—
everywhere springtime and the noise of birds,
a splatter of crocuses, hollyhocks by the gate,
wagtails darting into the lilac bush,
a gust of melancholy in the heart.

## A STATE OF GRACE

She walks in wearing nothing but talcum powder.
There is a sense of time drawing to an end,
of alternate lives conducted near the outer
edges of galaxies and worlds beyond,
of our own lonely bodies drying down
to nothing more than smudges on a thumb
rubbed clean against a pantleg in oblivion.
Her way of stepping under sweet perfume
between the open window and the bed
makes thought of any kind impertinent.
Too seldom is the wish to lie beside
the miracle of the world an element
in even the most immoderate likelihood
or the least part of something understood.

What Gauguin heard on the beach at Mataiea
was the voice of the planet out along the reef.
He lit a cigarette and looked away
toward the great black mountain. Where his life
had driven him thus far was nowhere near
as long from home as he was doomed to be,
though far enough for now. The mountain wore
what seemed to him a face of irony,
as if the answer to the question was
an altogether different kind of question
about the body being what it is—
an island in the middle of an ocean
moaning beyond its cold periphery
against the violet tedium of the sky.

3

## THE ROOMING HOUSE

Coming down from upstairs in his work clothes,
my father stands around as if he needs
permission to use the green chair in the living room.
Everything is ready for friends and relatives
of the woman whose house this is. She is in the kitchen,
carving the crusts off little sandwiches.
He leans against the doorway watching her,
then goes and sits and waits till the visitors
are entering the vestibule from the porch.
One is a woman in a foxtail coat.
She lifts it off and shakes out the snowflakes
from the blizzard whitening the bricks of the house
that the woman in the kitchen lets him keep
a room in, for the rest of all our lives.

I read this in the Gospel of St. John:
A difficult man, whose fondness for sarcasm
ran him afoul of the typical psychopaths
who always find careers in government,
got himself vilified, tortured, and nailed up,
while his mother stood by, gazing heavenward,
as the poor man squirmed and died, though not before
he had taken care of mother, who went on
to a long life in the comfort of her friends.
He should have seen it far enough ahead
to make sure he was safely out of town.
No matter that the onset comes before our time,
we get a lifetime for evasive action.
It's like my father told me in a letter:
"If things start closing in, just take a ride."
I took a ride, early this afternoon.
Brightness spilled over town and countryside.
When I drove back, I found my boy's new cat,
the one with the gray eyes, wandering in the road.
I brought her home. I gave her food. She slept
under a potted plant on the front porch.
Sometimes I need love's answer to the question
about the breathing creatures and their pain.
I shouldn't be comfortable with the easy one
that claims the very daylight is a sign
of transubstantial warmth among the stars—
though there was brightness over town and countryside.

Once I was back indoors, I sat and looked
at the sunbeams playing over the stones I keep
on my windowsill as souvenirs of oceans
that used to sing to me when I called them,
and for a while it seemed these stones were new,
still gleaming with Creation's primal flame
in the micromoment of transparent fire
when the Incandescent Mind had given thought
to Its desire. By the time I looked again
to bless my eyes with brittle bits of sun
through the clean rigor of the windowpane,
shadows had come on, and the light was gone
from nothing but a sill with a few stones.

Boethius says that sons are torturers,
quoting Euripides on the happiness
of childless men. Lady Philosophy
very simply answers him: pleasure brings pain,
presumably the pleasure of copulation,
the pain of childbirth and of rearing children,
especially sons. Boethius had sons,
who never came to visit him in prison,
or were away on business in the East,
or died as boys of something in the water.
Philosophy concludes with her cliché
about the honeybee: how it gives honey,
then leaves a sting to fester in our hearts.
I sit up late in a motel in Memphis
under a night-light reading this while he sleeps.
His breathing isn't anything like bees.
He said if he should wake before I do,
he'd stay there in the dark and wait for me.

Nobody seems to know what Jesus meant.
At least not me. I let the cat come in
to eat her dinner by the stereo
where Ashkenazy bends to his andante.
He seems to know exactly what Mozart meant.
The cat looks glad to have these bits to eat,
these keys of mercy struck above her ears
which tremble unbeknown at what they hear.
God knows I'm happy too, I know I am,
though nobody seems to know what Jesus meant.
I know I don't. I am compelled to watch
and listen here, more mystified than ever,
and not for lack of trying, even though
the pool of daylight by the cat's backside,
or the quiet after Vladimir quits the keys,
brings more beatitude than I could bear.

Father liked reading Wordsworth in the bathroom
in a great voice, pitching his vagrant tent
among the unfenced regions of his brain.
He hated Wordsworth like a pestilence.
One of his favorite tactics of derision
was to recite the Scriptures mockingly.
There was a tang of mockery in the air,
a vibrancy of mockery through the door.
Once he was at this long enough, maybe
the better part of a good hour or so,
another sound would rise amid the din
of his locution, curling onto it
and then all through it like a wisp of smoke,
as from another life we both had lived,
a bar in Ensenada where the beer
was kept in ice in buckets on the table
and the smoke hung like a blue veil over us,
wavering when she walked in from the street
to sit beside the window in the stillness
after the laughter and the songs died down.

Once Wordsworth dreamed he met a Bedouin
bearing a spear and, under one arm, a stone,
which the Bedouin said was Euclid's *Elements*.
A shell took the spear's place and then became
an emblem of something soothing to the spirit,
but Wordsworth couldn't tell about the stone
or why it had become some kind of book,
though soon he woke in a seacave with *Don Quixote*
open beside him, so Wordsworth said: "I see!
This shell is my prophetic Self; the stone
suggests a windmill grinding; I raise my spear
of poesy to strike against the mind's
impairment of the soul. I am the Bedouin,
the desert is the sea I slept beside
to dream this mighty dream." Later in Paris,
he slipped the button loose from the third hole
in the bodice of the nightgown Annette had on
one sultry night during the Revolution,
while the heavy spear he bore between his loins
presented itself to the shell she held in hers,
till all the other buttons tore loose and clattered
onto the floor like pebbles by the sea.
Then Wordsworth remembered the Bedouin, and saw
in one delirious spot of time on fire
a figure like a god astride the sunset
with a man before him prostrate, looking down

to where a broiling wheel throbbed in his eyes
and the smell of his own sweat steamed up from the dune,
which was her breastbone glistening under him.

In Proust's great work, *In Search of Wasted Time,*
there is a wonderful girl named Albertine
whose fruitlike breasts Proust often wants to fondle.
He contemplates the clothing of Albertine
containing Albertine and her impudent breasts.
He has in mind the ultimate paradise
of dozens of naked Albertines on a beach,
their dewy bodies glinting in morning light.

That Albertine was a man whom Proust adored
who wrecked his plane in the Atlantic Ocean
is certainly a fact worth mentioning.
This vision of Albertine in her chemise
can blossom forth to fill the mind with flesh
becoming spirit, which is a great thing,
whoever he or she may in fact have been
in time or out of time, in a cloak of skin.

## STICKBUG

There on the windowsill the dead walkingstick
is just as dead as he was last week. The children
come in to look him over and pronounce him strange,
or me strange, or both, for him being there
and for me keeping him the way I do,
neither of which can even begin to match
the general oddity of everything else
outside the glass he prances immovably by.
I am not confused about what should be done.
What's good for him is good for everyone.
The play of light, like the play of mind, anyone's mind,
mine or the children's or anyone else's,
on him by himself or him in the sun,
where he might leave a shadow on the sill
to make him seem more real and more alive,
amounts to what we choose to think it means,
though no one will call him a fool bug for being there
or the husk of a failed insect that ought to be
consigned to the trashcan or to the toilet bowl,
not to my face at least, or I swear I will
invite them to grasp the fierceness of his gait,
the dread panache with which he swaggers on his way
along the windowsill his footfalls subdue
like the last province of oblivion.

## GREAT BEAST

I dip a hand for snakes known to these weeds
to writhe around the floor beside my shoe.
Desperate enmities between a man
and lower forms of life should flake away.
Outside my window there, the grumbling crows
await their turns to take the air again
to tear it with their nasty blasphemies
and put it back together as a veil
of rags that wag and dangle in the breeze
their oily cries contaminate. The bird
I'd like to be if I could be a bird
would hiss and bark and curse at the same time,
a kind of man and crow and watersnake
with ragged wings that flapped but did not fly.

No dream that he remembered came to him.
He woke to mornings, one after the other,
with a clear head, the daylight clean as linen,
and the small talk of the birds to listen in on,
maybe the talk of workmen up the block
doing somebody's roof, or a new garage—
and this would leave him wishing he could think
the plain way they did, about daily things
unamplified by supple turns of phrase,
though after he had thought that out awhile
he slowly gained the strength of recognition
to admit his joy in how the words themselves
adorned the morning and repaired his soul
regardless of the psyche's dearth of dreams
and the birds' dearth of colorful grace notes
to which the ear could resonate despite
the lack of nuance in the song. Besides,
he kept forgetting what he'd come here for.
After awhile he could no more account
for why he sat here where you see him now
than he could tell you what the goldfinch thought
the instant she took the air beyond the birdbath
towering above that kindly garden there
with its red bench of simple planks and nails
upon a lawn of simpler greens and shadows
swaying from treelimbs raised against the sun

that was the village star, the local god,
a white blast from a trapdoor in a sky
filled with its dream of old things put away.

## LAWN MOWER

When I came out on the far end of the swath
exposed by the five-blade push-reel lawn mower
I had aimed in one direction till it reached
the fence that keeps my yard from my neighbor's woods,
I stopped and looked around at the green sea
with its wake of cuttings, and I asked myself
Why would you want to do a thing like that?
and then I stood the mower against the fence
and walked back up the path to the garage
where the boxes on the shelves along one wall
kept magazines and toys and hand-me-downs,
and the open sack of cow manure on the floor
held promise of more grass I would not mow
and on the windowsill the radio
played Copland's "Fanfare for the Common Man"
amidst a rubble of wirenuts and flathead screws.

## ANGELOLOGY

When Robert Grosseteste comments on the angels
and whether more than one might coexist
in the same place or body, he seems to think
such fine points are important because they test
the seriousness of our preoccupations,
in this case with the business of the spirit,
of spirits generally, and the spirit of God.
The main idea posits medial forms
between God and ourselves, and furthermore
appropriates the model of the soul
as mover of the body, coextensive
as the body and the soul appear to be,
supposing here the soul's reality,
which was hard to question in the thirteenth century,
though equally impossible to prove,
yet Robert argues the relationship
of angels to material elements
as casually as a man walking his dog,
showing us angels everywhere at once,
numberless angels all over the place
impinging on this world from the other world,
as the eye receives a vision of bare trees
mantled with mist, or the nostrils catch the savor
of a loved woman's delectable inner thigh
from mounds of mown grass in a stranger's yard.

Looking up as if to ask heaven for signs,
I noticed a blue as clean as a baby's sigh,
which I had known to expect, but even then
I only said I knew the things I saw,
and what I saw was empty of any signs,
as usual, which was itself a sign.
Whatever the vacant blue might be taken to mean
I left to colorists who cared for blue.
As for my own position under it,
flatly abstracted, with the neck bent back
to uphold a head pitched like a man-ape's skull
agog in the clay, I'd let anthroposophists,
those erstwhile friends who phone at 4 a.m.,
asseverate their notions, being as good
as any other cracked ideologues
at bringing truth to ground—it was all no more
than someone's name for someone else's fear
in an idiom no objection could gainsay.
What might be dangerous about such foolishness
was its capacity to win men over
to one immoderate claim on their convictions,
with no room left for any disbeliever.
My being here engaged in honest toil,
carefully hosing down the parched impatiens
so they might raise their sweet parts toward the sun
in glorious disregard of all the above,

confirmed my place as love's apologist,
and emissary from the vegetation,
in the unending war against the sky.

## TRUTH

Proust claimed truth is only a point of view
about things, which is as simple a refinement
on Augustine or Aquinas or Pascal
as anyone has come up with before or since.
This was a practical determination, entirely corrupt,
but far from theoretical or merely subjective.
Proust naturally had a novelist's motive
to get on with the story and to tell it well
from as many varying points of view
as he could imagine people to exhibit them.
Beyond that there was the esoteric,
if not the theological, aspect of it.
I wouldn't know much about either of those.
The truth is Proust couldn't know what the truth is,
certainly not now. And even in this life,
one of the few things he verified for sure
was the fact that one steeple viewed through the trees
has a different aspect from another steeple taken in
a few paces farther on up the lane,
which is your basic phenomenological program
given as a starting point in any history of ideas,
as well as an earthen vessel full of body waste
thoughtfully ingested by adenoidal pseudophilosophs,
whose ranks Proust was a micromillisecond's
fluctuation in a braincell away from
on any given day. Heartbreaking as it is,

truth belongs only to someone positively unlike Proust,
who knew the paths of time and how they lead
past doors the dead would open if they could.

# REQUIEM

At the end of the millennium, in the city of the dream,
is a backstreet emptying into a square
dominated by a church whose façade consists
entirely of a mosaic of Christ Judging the Damned
among golden glitter catching the sunset
from the river opposite
where the street turns into an esplanade
along the lake with its villas and boatclubs

though I am searching for the dead friend I ate with
in a beanery downtown at a table with green chairs
beneath the grimy portrait of Our Beloved Founder,
who, as a boy in Macedonia, watched from the rootcellar
the slaughter of his father, mother, and other townspeople
before he left with one tapestry satchel
to come here to stare through astonished spectacles
over bins of hotdogs covered with damp towels

at Kovac and me eating two with everything
before we head off for the old man's funeral
where everyone gets up from a clatter of folding chairs,
the men smoking pipes, the women hugging their purses,
the children taking their places like good little soldiers,
the patriarch dissolving under billows of incense,
and Kovac's wire-rims flickering from the doorway
as he darts out into the noonday glare.

He wrapped a hand around my right forefinger
and walked with me down the hill to the bus stop
by a broad boulevard under aching light.
We stepped inside a house with tinted windows.
Women in bathrobes moved from room to room.
A bus was coming down a corridor.
I left him waiting there and went back out
into the sunlight and on up the street
where I could see a prospect of the city
verging toward purple hills and turquoise sky.
A cul-de-sac in the shadows to one side
invited me down to the doorsill of an inn.
The air hung thick with essence of lavender
among egret feathers in the cool vestibule.

The innkeeper's wife ran in from the dining room
and turned around once on her tiny heels.
She saw me from the middle of her turn.
I was explaining how unblameworthy I was,
since all I came for was to find my way
out of this place, nice as it happened to be
and pleasant as all my memories ever after
would certainly seem to my clear inner eye,
though all I wanted now was a route of egress
by some means through that back wall over there
so I could take my leave and make my way

back up the hill I came down earlier,
leaving my mother at the restaurant
with ivory fingers folded on the table.

A woman sits at a table by the wall.
The waiter brings a plate of octopus
and a beaker of cool wine. The air is full
of jasmine, and the woman's skin is sweet
as the flowers of jasmine leaning by her chair
from the potted bush beside it. Glorious
simplicity abounds in the sun's glare
from the wall her shadow seems to have stained
like the body's interruption of the mind
when the mind has begun to come upon the truth
about our ordinary lives on earth,
while here before it, in the least of places,
beauty is breathing in and breathing out
and watching the rest of us watching her
like so many imbeciles with dreaming faces.

## BADIA FIESOLANA

No sooner had the blue air over the garden
become pearlescent in the spindly trees

than I perceived a cloud bank rolling in
to take me from a backroad near Fiesole

where my good friend and I went walking
with our walking sticks beside pastel villas

and we said the lovely women that we knew
must likewise find us lovely, though we were not,

and I could only imagine why God would make
these women crazy enough to love us the way they did—

two young men waxing old on our walking sticks,
two crazed swains lurching off along the road

to view the tombs in the Badia Fiesolana
and run our fingers over polished stones

that took our breath away and made us sigh out loud,
What is this love we carry to our graves?

Those blessed habitats around the yard,
where the brain misplaces oddments of former lives,
can gleam with rare decorum, suddenly,
lifting you out of ordinary time,
so you can find out how you came to be here
when the mild old gentleman in the broad plaid coat
reached for a breath while hurrying up to give you
another recollection from the War,
hardly betraying the least canniness
about the world's way or his own life even,
itself for him merely an incident
in a series of discontiguous events
involving other men more praiseworthy,
which is the unavoidable inference
the mind absorbs from what he rubbed his jaw
to offer, seeming all the while a man
of customary breadth and easy wherewithal,
a veritable banquet of a human being,
though all left over, but for what he tells,
or thinks he does, of what he used to be,
until the fatal pause arrives to part you,
releasing you to others, who will come
awash in afternoon bedazzlements
to pluck you from that region of the soul
into another where the daylilies
pretend advanced conditions of aplomb.
It seldom ever is a different way.

After the last insouciant departure,
the scented air falls cool and affable.
A measured crunch of footfalls up the path
precedes the dreadful visitation:
almost as if a voice from the other side
had garbled messages to breathe to you,
you turn your ear intently toward the news
a man and woman strolling amiably
among the pale green shadows of the roadway
intimate barely audibly between them
before you note your own voice crying out.
Once, in what really was another time,
they were your fellow voyagers abroad,
gaining the corner by the Swan Hotel,
briskly materializing above cobblestones
among half-timbered shopfronts, gabled roofs,
the fabulous lost quarter at the end
of the last block in the town within a town
you always knew was there. A lambency
of afternoon suffused the white façade
of the cathedral, with its towers alike
except for billboards on the northernmost
extolling virtues various and timely
against a sky patrolled by silver birds
in tight-knit teams of no more than five each
leaping in gusty bolts across the blue,
while here below a priest in overalls

and Roman collar knelt to his flower garden
beside the campanile, his forehead flecked
with glints of bloom. His mind was orchid-light
breaking upon the darkness he understood
as deity but never could divulge
to the immediate neighborhood, so gave
his mind to bee and blossom, leaf and jay,
his broken heart consoled by lonely joy
of abject reckoning, while the comforter
visited someone else, he told himself,
if only to believe that this could be,
which was no small thing for the likes of him,
and as for that one who was comforted,
he prayed to learn from intercourse of spirits,
once they attained their mutual paradise,
what earthly bliss was like, if they had power
to recollect it from that timeless quiet
so like the calm that dropped from stopping bells
till pigeons lit along the ledge again
to peck above him poking at the ground.
The circumambulation of the soul
would have been like that, bringing to the heart
the rise of blood that comes from other life
discovered suddenly, the way you round
a corner to a place you knew of old,
the innkeeper and his young wife sitting down
to take a bit of brandy with the couple

who spent the whole day at the doll museum
in Winchester in a lane near the Cathedral.
It was the sadness in their eyes that haunted her,
their looks of frozen longing, while for him
it was the pathos in the way these people gave
their daughters little statues instead of love,
to touch our hearts in the next century
with dimpled fingers reaching from lacy sleeves,
their empty hands uplifted. Having said so,
he raised cigar and snifter in one fist
to catch the firelight like a leaping bird
or like a child's face crying from the glass
to be delivered. At the sight of that,
the four of them lapsed into silences
composed of memories unique to each,
the meaning of which was lost on one and all.
Fragrant with widowed aunts and morning glories,
a gorgeous wildness kept its own domain
in the next block over. Patrick, the Airedale,
tapped off along the hall toward the vestibule
to lie down with a shudder and a sigh,
an equilibrium having set in
so all were satisfied to be where they were
or to go elsewhere if it could be done
over an ocean of equanimity
covered with islands whose interiors

kept villages of corrugated roofs
and bougainvillea that the black goats browse
miles above captains in the anchorage.

## THE IOWA POETRY PRIZE WINNERS

1 9 8 7
Elton Glaser, *Tropical Depressions*
Michael Pettit, *Cardinal Points*

1 9 8 8
Bill Knott, *Outremer*
Mary Ruefle, *The Adamant*

1 9 8 9
Conrad Hilberry, *Sorting the Smoke*
Terese Svoboda, *Laughing Africa*

1 9 9 3
Tom Andrews, *The Hemophiliac's Motorcycle*
Michael Heffernan, *Love's Answer*
John Wood, *In Primary Light*

## THE EDWIN FORD PIPER POETRY AWARD WINNERS

1 9 9 0
Philip Dacey, *Night Shift at the Crucifix Factory*
Lynda Hull, *Star Ledger*

1 9 9 1
Greg Pape, *Sunflower Facing the Sun*
Walter Pavlich, *Running near the End of the World*

1 9 9 2
Lola Haskins, *Hunger*
Katherine Soniat, *A Shared Life*